Henley-on-Thames

A little souvenir

CHRIS ANDREWS PUBLICATIONS

Introduction to Henley on Thames

A settlement was first established at this river crossing in the twelfth century. Henley has has always been a busy place with good transport links; for many years it was a port supplying timber, corn and malt to London. In the eighteenth century it was an important coaching post, and with the coming of the Great Western Railway in 1857 Henley grew still further.

Now it is an affluent commuter town. Beside the majestic eighteenth century bridge is The Angel pub, held by Cromwell's men during the Civil War. The Red Lion once gave lodgings to Charles I; and Prince Rupert is said to have hanged a spy on a tree known as "Rupert's Elm".

Henley has many interesting architectural details and buildings, including the Chantry House, just behind the church. It is the town's only Grade 1 listed building, some 500

The Angel, Henley Bridge and the Church of St Mary The Virgin   5

6 Chantry House interior

years old and was extensively renovated in the early 2000's. It is largely used as church offices.

Henley is perhaps best known for its Royal Regatta, a major social event that takes over the town for the 27th week of each year. Rowing crews come from all over the world to race along possibly the best stretch of river in Britain. In 1829 the first boat race between Oxford and Cambridge took place here; ten years later Henley launched its annual regatta. Prince Albert became the first patron in 1851 and the regatta acquired its Royal prefix.

Unpredictable Regatta weather

The first regatta was over in three hours; today preparations for the event start in April and the races are on five days of July followed by a week's art and music festival. There are striking contrasts between the competing crews and the formally dressed guests.

For the majority of people this colourful pageant has more to do with champagne and strawberries than physical prowess and the river.

10 Henley Royal Regatta headquarters

Early morning, the tow path at Mill Meadows   11

12   Launches for Regatta umpires moored south of the bridge

14   Dusk on the river

16 Malthouse towers of the old brewery and the Town Hall

Inside the former brewery, now a noted hotel   17

18   A variety of Henley rooftops

The Kenton Theatre, built in 1805 is the 4th oldest working theatre in the country   19

20   Riverside houses above Marsh Lock

A converted boathouse below Marsh Lock 21

22 Temple Island, used by The Regatta but built as a fishing lodge for Fawley Court by James Wyatt

The view from the bridge

26   The footway leading to Marsh Lock

Early winter morning and a mist on the river below the Town   27

28 Woodlands surrounding Henley

Winter view south from the bridge   29

30   The riverside in winter

Sculptures of Sir Steve Redgrave and Sir Mathew Pinsent at The River & Rowing Museum   31

32   The award winning River & Rowing Museum

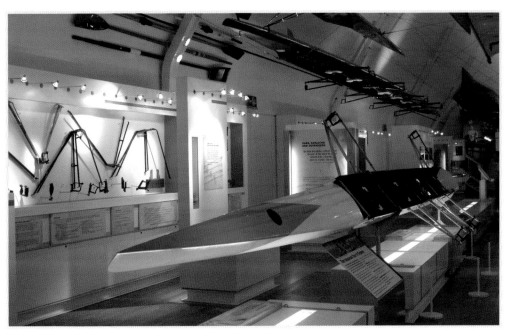

The Museum's Rowing Gallery featuring the winning Sydney Olympic IV   33

34   Leander is the world's oldest rowing club, founded in 1818

Henley Royal Regatta standard, flying from the headquarters on the bridge　35

36   Henley from the south east, with the Regatta tents on the nearside river bank

Leisure boats for hire and the Regatta course   37

38   Pre-race preparation in the boat tents showing 1980's oar design

Lower part of the Regatta course and the Town

42   A racing eight and the boat tents

The Course, 1 mile 550 yards, viewed from the church tower   43

44   A ladies eight in training at the start of the course. the Regatta has been mixed since 1988

46　Quadruple sculls at the beginning of the race

48   Waterborne spectators line the lower part of the course

On the banks of the Regatta enclosure 49

50   The final push in an early race

52   Rowing continues throughout the day

Steward's enclosure and refreshment, for some   53

54   The Traditional Boat Rally started in 1977 and follows Henley Festival

56   The River Thames and bridge from just above the church

58   Henley Festival of Music and the Arts follows the Regatta

60   The Festival runs for a week from early evening to night

62   Festival seating in the evening

First published 2005

Reprinted 2011

Chris Andrews Publications Ltd, 15 Curtis Yard, North Hinksey Lane, Oxford, OX2 0NA

Telephone: +44(0)1865 723404 email: enquiries@cap-ox.com Photos by Chris Andrews

ISBN 978-1-095385-02-7

All material © Chris Andrews Publications Ltd

Designed and produced by Chris Andrews. Originated by Butler and Tanner. Printed in Singapore

www.cap-ox.com

All rights reserved. No part of this publication may be reproduced, stored in a retrieval system, or transmitted, in any form or by any means, without prior permission of the copyright holder. The right of Chris Andrews as author of this work have been asserted by him in accordance with the Copyright, Designs and Patents Act 1988

Acknowledgement: Thanks to The River & Rowing Museum and Henley TIC for all help and encouragement

Front Cover: The Thames and Henley Bridge

Title: 'Isis' by Anne Damar

Back cover: Riverside Houses